W9-BIA-942

LAND OF THE SKY

LAND OF THE SKY

WONDERS OF THE BLUE RIDGE AND GREAT SMOKY MOUNTAINS

PETER BENEY

LONGSTREET PRESS
Atlanta, Georgia

Published by
LONGSTREET PRESS, INC.
2150 Newmarket Parkway
Suite 102
Marietta, Georgia 30067

Printed in Hong Kong

1st printing, 1990

Library of Congress Catalog Card Number: 89-063791

ISBN 0-929264-29-0

This book was printed in Hong Kong by Everbest Printing Company, Ltd., through Four Color Imports, Ltd. The text was set in Palatino by Typo-Repro Service, Inc., Atlanta, Georgia. Cover design by Laura Ellis.

To my mother and father
for their encouragement

LAND OF THE SKY

The Appalachians, the oldest mountains in the United States, stretch from Maine to Georgia — a broad ribbon of numerous parallel ranges joined by cross ranges and tumbled mountains and hills. The mountains themselves are ancient and rugged; their coves and valleys are deep and narrow.

By far the most beloved and most visited portion of this ancient chain is the stretch running from northern Virginia into Georgia, dominated by the Blue Ridge and Great Smoky Mountains, but also including the Black Mountains, the Craggies, Pisgahs, and Balsams. These mountains, hills, coves, and valleys have been home to courageous native Americans, sturdy and resourceful Scotch-Irish immigrants, and captains of American industry.

Today, Cherokees preserve their traditions and culture on a reservation just outside the Great Smoky Mountains National Park. Descendants of those original Scotch-Irish settlers still populate the area and keep alive their ancestors' music, religion, and love of the challenging terrain and majestic beauty of this adopted homeland. And George Vanderbilt's legacy lives on as well, in the grandeur of Biltmore House, his Asheville, North Carolina, estate and in his lasting contribution to the preservation of the area's natural beauty. The acres Vanderbilt accumulated and managed as part of his estate became one of the first tracts of the Pisgah National Forest.

Across the top of this massive stretch of mountains, the Blue Ridge Parkway runs for almost five hundred miles, connecting the Shenandoah National Park in northern Virginia with the Great Smoky Mountains National Park that sprawls across the border between North Carolina and Tennessee. It is a major artery, carrying millions of tourists each year into the heart of one of the country's most beautiful and most breathtaking natural treasures.

As early as 1872, Americans were praising the glories of the region in print. In *Picturesque America*, a magazine edited by the renowned poet William Cullen Bryant, an article on the region dominated by the French Broad River, which runs through Asheville, North Carolina, used the phrase "land of the sky" in an effort to capture the immensity of the place and the inescapable feeling that nature is omnipresent, right there for visitors to reach out and touch. Frances Christine Tiernan (nee Fisher) in 1876 published a book under the pen name Christian Reid. She called it *Land of the Sky*, a phrase that came to her when, on a stagecoach trip to Asheville, she passed Mount Mitchell and Mount Pisgah at dawn. Looking out upon the majestic wonders before her, she was overcome by the rapturous beauty and exclaimed, "Dear God, I thank thee for this thy gift, the land of the sky."

For more than a century, visitors to the Blue Ridge and Great Smoky Mountains have shared her sentiment. Even earlier, visitors to the region were equally moved, for Mount Pisgah is named for the biblical mountain from which Moses beheld the promised land. The mountains of the Blue Ridge and Great Smokies are still a land of great promise for any visitor who seeks to explore their wonders. **Land of the Sky** is a sampling of what awaits, along their surface and deep within their mysterious soul.

Smoky Mountains from Foothills Parkway, Tennessee

LOOKING GLASS ROCK, NORTH CAROLINA

Autumn oak, Blue Ridge Parkway overlooking Great Smoky
Mountains National Park, Tennessee

WATER MILL NEAR COSBY, TENNESSEE

MORNING SUNLIGHT, SOUTH CAROLINA

FALLS ON LITTLE RIVER, TOWNSEND END OF LITTLE RIVER ROAD, TENNESSEE

GREAT SMOKY MOUNTAINS NATIONAL PARK FROM CLINGMAN'S DOME, NORTH CAROLINA-TENNESSEE LINE

DOGWOOD

BULL SLUICE, CHATTOOGA RIVER, ON ROUTE 76 AT GEORGIA-SOUTH CAROLINA LINE

Shenandoah River, Harper's Ferry, Virginia

SNOW IN SHENANDOAH, VIRGINIA

Pink dawn in the Smoky Mountains, North Carolina

Autumn maple, North Carolina

ABOVE: TOBACCO IN TENNESSEE

RIGHT: SMOKY MOUNTAINS, NORTH CAROLINA

SPACE NEEDLE, GATLINBURG, TENNESSEE

Shenandoah River, Harper's Ferry, Virginia

Sunset in Soco Gap, Blue Ridge Parkway, North Carolina

REDBUDS IN TENNESSEE

19

Fungi in North Carolina

Autumn woods in North Carolina

Sunset over foothills, Tellico Lake, Tennessee

View from Brasstown Bald, near Blairsville, Georgia

MEADOW RUN GRIST MILL, NEAR CHARLOTTESVILLE, VIRGINIA

CHILHOWEE MOUNTAINS, LITTLE RIVER, GREAT SMOKY MOUNTAINS NATIONAL PARK, TENNESSEE

Virginia creeper on Little River, Great Smoky Mountains National Park, Tennessee

Falls near Townsend, Great Smoky Mountains National Park, Tennessee

ABOVE: FENCE IN WINTER AT OCONOLUFTEE VISITOR CENTER AND PIONEER FARMSTEAD, NEAR OCONOLUFTEE RANGER STATION, NORTH CAROLINA

LEFT: WOODEN FENCE AT OCONOLUFTEE VISITOR CENTER

FALLS AT ROCK CITY, NEAR CHATTANOOGA, TENNESSEE

Mount Pisgah, Blue Ridge Mountains, North Carolina

Appalachian Trail, near Neel's Gap, Georgia

LITTLE RIVER, GREAT SMOKY MOUNTAINS NATIONAL PARK

SUNSET AT GRAVEYARD FIELDS, BLUE RIDGE PARKWAY, NORTH CAROLINA

Mabry Mill, Blue Ridge Parkway near North Carolina-Virginia line, Virginia

DOGWOODS IN AUTUMN, NORTH CAROLINA

Looking Glass Falls, Pisgah National Forest, North Carolina

PUMPKINS IN GEORGIA

FARM AT GROUNDHOG MOUNTAIN, BLUE RIDGE PARKWAY, VIRGINIA

SNOWY FIRS, BLUE RIDGE MOUNTAINS, NORTH CAROLINA

MOON OVER SMOKY MOUNTAINS, TENNESSEE

ABOVE: CANTILEVER BARN, CADES COVE

LEFT: CADES COVE, GREAT SMOKY MOUNTAINS NATIONAL PARK, TENNESSEE

SNOW ON TREES, BLUE RIDGE MOUNTAINS, NORTH CAROLINA

SUNSET OVER BLUE RIDGE MOUNTAINS, NORTH CAROLINA

Dogwood trees, Great Smoky Mountains National Park, near Gatlinburg, Tennessee

CARTER SHIELDS CABIN, CADES COVE, GREAT SMOKY MOUNTAINS NATIONAL PARK, TENNESSEE

BLUE DAWN, SMOKY MOUNTAINS, NORTH CAROLINA

RHODODENDRONS, NEAR CRAGGY GARDENS, NORTH CAROLINA

Dry Falls, between Highlands and Franklin, North Carolina

THE CHIMNEYS, GREAT SMOKY MOUNTAINS NATIONAL PARK, TENNESSEE

BILTMORE HOUSE, ASHEVILLE, NORTH CAROLINA

Autumn stream in North Carolina

MINGO FALLS, NEAR CHEROKEE, NORTH CAROLINA

Maggie Valley, North Carolina

Above: Primitive Baptist Church, Cades Cove, Great Smoky Mountains National Park, Tennessee

Right: Winter, Blue Ridge Mountains, North Carolina

Old Mill of Pigeon Forge, Pigeon Forge, Tennessee

Tobacco, Route 321, between Maryville and Townsend, Tennessee

HOUSE IN SMOKY MOUNTAINS, NORTH CAROLINA

BRIDAL VEIL FALLS, BETWEEN HIGHLANDS AND FRANKLIN, NORTH CAROLINA

Mingus Mill on Oconaluftee River, Great Smoky Mountains National Park, North Carolina

GREAT SMOKY MOUNTAINS NATIONAL PARK, TENNESSEE

FOOT BRIDGE, SMOKY MOUNTAINS, ON ROAD BETWEEN
MARYVILLE AND TOWNSEND, TENNESSEE

Smokemont Bridge, near Cherokee Indian Reservation, North Carolina

GRIST MILL, NEAR CHEROKEE, NORTH CAROLINA

ICICLES, BLUE RIDGE PARKWAY, NORTH CAROLINA

LITTLE PIGEON RIVER, BETWEEN PIGEON FORGE AND GATLINBURG, TENNESSEE

MOUNTAIN LAUREL

ABOVE: DAFFODILS IN SOUTH CAROLINA

RIGHT: DAWN IN SMOKY MOUNTAINS, NORTH CAROLINA

Lick Log Mill near Highlands, North Carolina

LOWER FALLS, GRAVEYARD FIELDS, BLUE RIDGE PARKWAY, NORTH CAROLINA

MIST OVER LOOKING GLASS ROCK, PISGAH NATIONAL FOREST, NORTH CAROLINA

Skyline Drive, Shenandoah National Park, Virginia

Winter on Little River, Great Smoky Mountains National Park, Tennessee

CANTRELL CREEK LODGE, CRADLE OF FORESTRY OF AMERICA, PISGAH NATIONAL FOREST, NORTH CAROLINA

ROUTE 441 FROM NEWFOUND GAP, GREAT SMOKY MOUNTAINS NATIONAL PARK, NORTH CAROLINA-TENNESSEE LINE

SUNSET OVER FARM, SHENANDOAH VALLEY, NEW MARKET, VIRGINIA

BLUE RIDGE MOUNTAINS, NORTH CAROLINA

GLEN FALLS, HIGHLANDS, NORTH CAROLINA

SNOW IN SOCO GAP, BLUE RIDGE PARKWAY, NORTH CAROLINA

Grist mill, near Norris Dam, Tennessee

ABOVE: LOW WINTER SUN OVER MAGGIE VALLEY, NORTH CAROLINA

LEFT: BLUE RIDGE MOUNTAINS, NORTH CAROLINA

TOBACCO FARM, SMOKY MOUNTAINS, TENNESSEE

Upper Falls, Graveyard Fields, Blue Ridge Parkway, North Carolina

Observation Tower at Clingman's Dome, North Carolina-Tennessee line

Blue Ridge Mountains, from Blue Ridge Parkway, North Carolina

SUNRISE OVER FARM, SHENANDOAH VALLEY, NEW MARKET,
VIRGINIA

Farm in Tennessee

ABOVE: FROST IN SOUTH CAROLINA

RIGHT: RHODODENDRONS, NEAR CRAGGY GARDENS, NORTH CAROLINA

Amicalola Falls, near Dahlonega, Georgia

OCONOLUFTEE RIVER, CHEROKEE INDIAN RESERVATION, NORTH CAROLINA

SUNRISE, SMOKY MOUNTAINS, NORTH CAROLINA

Oconoluftee Pioneer Farmstead, near Oconoluftee Ranger Station, Great Smoky Mountains National Park, North Carolina

Blue Ridge Mountains, North Carolina

Oconoluftee River, Great Smoky Mountains National Park,
North Carolina

Mist on Blue Ridge Parkway, North Carolina

Peter Beney is the author of *Old South, National Parks of the U.S.,* and *Atlanta: A Brave and Beautiful City.* He lives in Roswell, Georgia.

Original custom photographic prints of the pictures in this book may be ordered from

The River Gallery
Centre Stage Shopping Mall
6050 Peachtree Parkway
Norcross, Georgia 30092
Telephone (404) 662-8865

Prices

11″ × 14″	Unmounted in tube	$95.00 each
11″ × 14″	Mounted, double-matted, signed, in 16″ × 20″ frame	$175.00 each
16″ × 20″	Unmounted in tube	$135.00 each
16″ × 20″	Mounted, double-matted, signed, in 20″ × 26″ frame	$245.00 each

Packing and shipping included for U.S. only

Quantity	Page Number	Description	Size	Tube or Frame	Price
_____	_____	_____	_____	_____	$_____
_____	_____	_____	_____	_____	$_____
_____	_____	_____	_____	_____	$_____
_____	_____	_____	_____	_____	$_____
			Georgia residents must include 5% sales tax		$_____
				Total	$_____

Allow 4 to 6 weeks for delivery

☐ I enclose check/money order payable to The River Gallery for $_____.

Charge my   ☐ MasterCard   ☐ Visa   ☐ American Express   ☐ Discover

Account number ☐ ☐ ☐ ☐ ☐ ☐ ☐ ☐ ☐ ☐ ☐ ☐ ☐ ☐ ☐ ☐

Expiration date _____ Signature _____

Name _____

Address _____

City _____ State _____ Zip _____